How to Live Life

Jean-Jacques Trifault

FOOTSTEPS TO WISDOM PUBLISHING

Copyright © 2012 by Jean-Jacques Trifault

Other books by Jean-Jacques Trifault:

Everything is a Gift
God is in My Heart
Gratitude to the Creation
An Open Heart Comes from an Open Mind
Can We Be the Gift for Someone?
Among Those Born of Women There was None Greater Than John
The Body of Christ
The Rebirth of God and Lisa
(Several books are translated into French and Spanish.)

To order books, please visit the author's website:
www.footstepstowisdom.org

ISBN: 978-0-9847433-1-5

Cover design and book layout by Kasia Krawczyk

Within every human being there is a deep quest to find truth. Some people believe they have found some truth, like religious people or people who have developed a certain philosophy. However when we look more closely, we will see that these people have a hard time to maintain and uphold their faith in their beliefs, as well as to follow what they believe is true.

Why do we look for truth? What is the goal of truth? Truth shows us the purpose of our lives and helps us to gain a greater awareness of our personal lifestyle in order to achieve a better life.

Most of us cannot easily find our purpose or our origin in the cosmic creation we live in. One main reason is because our eyes can only perceive the external or the physical side of what exists around us, which is the effect. An effect is usually easier to perceive than an origin or a cause because it is more visible. For example, it is easier to observe the effect than the cause of our body's behavior. Let's say we decide to rise early in the morning, but we find ourselves waking up later than we planned. After this event we do not feel so well, which is a feeling that represents the effect, but its cause was that we could not fulfill our desire to rise early, regardless it was due to various reasons, like our body felt we were too tired or it was still dark outside and we turned off the alarm clock. Now let's say we wake up early, accomplishing our wish. In this case we experience contentment as the effect, while our motivation to rise early and our success in fulfilling our desire stand as the cause.

In fact, there is a cause and effect relationship in the midst of every thought, behavior and feeling we can have. Can we imagine how many cause and effect relationships there are in one day of our life, if we consider the vast realms of thoughts, actions and feelings?

When we have a sickness we can identify this condition as being the effect. We have the tendency to perceive the effect first because the symptoms of the sickness have the attribute of being more visible than its cause. But when we go to see a doctor, his first instinct will be to try to find the cause of the sickness, because then he will know how to treat it.

This is similar to the focus of religious leaders, who also are concerned about human beings' problems, but on a more internal level. Like doctors, they look for the cause of human beings' characteristics, which they call the 'soul'.

Therefore, if we want to understand the characteristics of human beings, which are the effects, we will need to research their causes. In general we can say a good cause, or origin, creates beauty in human beings, whereas a destructive cause has the ability to create ugliness. Since most of us want to be considered as beautiful, or in other words, as human beings of love, we will have to find a truth that promotes the cause that creates goodness, also called the viewpoint of goodness or God's viewpoint. Once we have discovered this kind of truth, we can direct our body toward a life of goodness.

Since most of us want to be considered as beautiful human beings of love, we will have to find a truth that creates goodness.

The effect of finding and accepting this truth or this viewpoint of goodness is that it gives our mind breadth and stability, while rejecting this truth and choosing the way of ignorance and selfishness makes our mind narrow, weak and unstable. The main property of the viewpoint of goodness is that it teaches us to welcome life and to welcome people; in other words, it directs us to harmonize ourselves with everything around us and to stay positive about events that arrive to our lives.

How We Choose to Respond

Regardless we can find some thought that we can identify as being good, like wanting to welcome others, this does not guarantee that it will be easy for us to maintain that thought in the midst of our daily lives. Let's take the example of somebody calling us the worst person in the world. How will we react? Our choice of response depends upon the philosophy we have learned to use for ourselves. One possibility is to reject this person's statement and to counter-attack him. Another possibility is to accept what he says, in other words, to humble ourselves. To achieve humility, in this case we might choose to answer, "Yes, maybe I am the worst person in the world. Thank you so much to tell me, I didn't know that. But now I know and I can do something to change it." This is one of the best ways to think.

Yet most people will question why that person criticized them. It is normal to feel bad about being criticized. But to remove that feeling of unpleasantness, our tendency is to deny the accusation instead of humbling ourselves to the criticism. For this reason we usually accuse the person in return by pointing out some weak point in him, believing we will be free from feeling bad. Another way to respond is to tell ourselves that what was said is not true and that we are not so bad after all. Either way attempts to cover the negative feelings the remark created in us, but will have the effect of creating a whirlpool inside our emotions.

Every human being will try to use some technique or philosophy to remove the painful feeling caused by an accusation. A person's choice will depend on who we think we are. If we are a person of low self esteem, the tendency is to accuse others when they accuse us so we can feel good again. If we have high self-esteem, we will give extra praise to ourselves to regain our sense of value and to be able to ignore the one who accused us.

Let me give some more examples about these two categories of persons. Seen from the concept of cause and effect, if we don't believe we are good, even just one negative word coming to us can cause us to feel depressed, as the effect. If we have the tendency to have high self esteem, we might feel so surprised about what somebody says to us because it is in contradiction to what we believe we are.

We have a personality of goodness within ourselves that drives us to act unselfishly in order to become divine one day.

In the category of low self-esteem, people believe they are bad and that they are destined to stay bad, or believe they just have bad fortune and everything they attempt to do will not succeed. On the side of high self-esteem, people believe that they are good and must be trusted. Regardless of our category of thought, each thought represents the cause, in consideration of our response as the effect.

Whatever side we think we are, if we are sincere we will acknowledge that the most objective viewpoint is to recognize that we have both good and bad points in ourselves. If everyone can use this viewpoint, then whatever thought they had about themselves, as being either a good or a bad person, will be transformed into a more balanced thought, which will create a new cause with a new effect.

We need to remember that due to our self-centeredness we are going to find ourselves acting selfishly in various ways, and because of this nature we can say we are impure or not yet the divine human beings we were meant to be. At the same time we need to recognize that we have a personality of goodness within ourselves, and that this personality drives us to act unselfishly in order to become divine one day.

A Personality of Goodness or of Selfishness

If we can strive to live according to our personality of goodness, we will find new characteristics developing. These characteristics will open themselves to us according to how much we pursue the way of unselfishness in our lives. Yet even as we find more and more beautiful parts inside us, we need to keep the awareness that we still have elements of a bad self inside of us. As our goodness starts to be more dominant than our selfishness, we will tend to believe that there is no longer anything in us that can be judged as being bad. We need to learn to maintain a certain objectivity toward ourselves, without over-estimating or under-estimating our goodness or our selfishness.

There are origins to the good and bad natures inside of us. By all means, they didn't come about by accident.

We inherited them from history and then directly from our parents, making us the last link in the line of our ancestry. If we choose a thought that promotes selfishness as the cause of our behavior, we will develop our selfishness even more and oppress what is good or unselfish in us. But if we choose a thought that promotes goodness or unselfishness, this thought will have the power to remove the nature of selfishness. So we can say these two natures can grow inside us according to the thought we choose as the cause of our behavior.

Most of us refuse to sincerely look at ourselves, just because it might be painful. Therefore we are unaware of the causes of our actions and feelings. We are confused to the point where we say to ourselves or to others that whatever we are is what we are and nobody can change that.

Due to this reality we carry so many contradictions inside us. We find life so complicated and start to question everything. But instead of questioning why somebody said something to us, for instance, we can choose to be grateful to the person who made some remark to us, since through his or her words we can perceive our reaction and it can help us to understand ourselves. By choosing to follow the way of goodness, which is to receive instead of to reject or question whatever comes to us, we grow the goodness inside of us.

This is the holy way of life. We should never question why events come to our lives. Instead, we should try to find some positive thought or action to pass through each situation, without isolating ourselves. If we question every event that comes to us in order to defend ourselves from what can hurt us or from what seems to be difficult, we will develop the side of ourselves that always makes us feel we are victims.

Perhaps we might feel that to live with this welcoming attitude is not realistic. But we will find, if we can seek to live a life of goodness, that we can adapt and our lives will develop many different flavors. Our attitude can promote goodness and happiness in our lives or it can destroy them. The difference lies in what we choose: if we reject what comes to us or if we accept the circumstances of our lives with grateful minds. For example, every day there is something that we could call a problem. But instead, we can interpret this so-called problem as a situation that can create something new in us.

> Whatever happens, we should say
> to ourselves, this is just the way
> life presents itself - and what can
> I do to live with this situation?

So, let's hope the thought we choose to act upon can promote harmony with others and with life around us. The best way is not to question what is behind what people tell us, but instead to welcome their words. We should not waste our time asking why a situation is coming to us, but instead invest our time to accept the events that arise.

The wisest way is to not question what life gives to us or why a person acts a certain way towards us, because the more we question the more we will create problems. Problems don't arise from reality but instead from within our minds. We should say to ourselves, whatever happens, "This is just the way life presents itself." And when we can perceive life this way, then a second attitude will emerge: "What can I do to live with this situation?"

Trust Others and Ourselves

The answer to many situations is not to reprimand or to correct the people around us according to the way we wish them to be, trying to make them do what we like or say what we like to hear. Instead, the best way is to learn to live with every person and situation we meet in our lives. By doing so we will become able to embrace life the way it comes to us.

I perceive that many people fight life with the belief that they can control life. Therefore it becomes their talent to reject whatever comes to them and they develop many thoughts concerning what is good or bad for them. This causes them, unknowingly or knowingly, to reject many opportunities that arise in their lives. As I am explaining this process, I am not even speaking about accepting very difficult situations, instead I am talking about the many little situations people encounter everyday with their friends, their husbands, their wives, or their children.

We cannot be happy if we reject life, which presents itself through thousands of different events. These events are like waves breaking upon a beach every day, in different forms and strengths. But does the beach reject the waves, even though the waves cause the beach to change shape? Therefore, what is the reason we do not accept life as it comes to us?

Events are like waves breaking upon a beach every day, in different forms and strengths. But does the beach reject the waves, even though the waves cause the beach to change shape?

One of the major reasons is that we cannot trust ourselves or others to handle situations. Maybe we already made a negative statement inside us, by saying to ourselves that we wouldn't be able to accept this or that situation, even before it was physically manifested. Therefore, just by imagining some situation, we can already feel a negative effect to the point we will reject in advance whatever might come to us.

Let's use an example. Imagine our child comes to us and asks if he can invite another child to our home. I believe most of us will respond to our child by asking who this other child is and why our child wants to bring someone in our home. Or, we might just say no to him in a matter of seconds, because it was the answer that came to us first. And if we do not say no in this case, let's say our child asks us if he can bring ten people at once. Surely we will already panic even at the thought. Because of this attitude, it is not easy for us to accept life.

It is interesting that we produce a word like 'no' even before an event is actualized. This proves that inside of us there is a certain kind of negative mind that creates something like a wall that blocks whatever tries to approach us—for instance, all different kinds of new ideas. Since new ideas arise anyway, whether we want them or not, we are guaranteed to experience conflict in our mind.

Therefore the question is, how do we overcome this negative characteristic that we carry inside us? The best way is to believe that we can learn new thoughts and grow through the things that happen to us. If we have this attitude, we will be surprised to find ourselves being able to accept and to adjust to every kind of situation.

In order to act upon an idea, we need to trust and to believe in ourselves. Trusting ourselves comes foremost from learning to believe in God or in an origin of goodness. After we learn to believe in God, we will find ourselves trusting life and therefore more easily welcoming daily events.

Unfortunately, many of our choices promote negativity towards life, causing us to go against new events, against something we never heard of or did before. Most people live with some ideology or concept inside their heads that makes them decide beforehand what they can and cannot do. They arrive at the point where they find themselves uttering, "I can't do this," a sentence that is well-known around the world.

Let's use a simple example. A father wants to have a picnic with his family in the park instead of having lunch at home. But the mother says, "Well, this is too complicated. We need to prepare ourselves as well as the children. Besides, I didn't shop for picnic food." What the father asks is indeed something good, seen from the viewpoint of wanting to create something different. It is just a simple event, meant to enhance the day. But when we look at the response of the mother, we can recognize her pessimism. Her multitude of answers block the possibility of carrying out that idea. If her mind were more optimistic, she would find a way to manage everything even though they didn't make a plan in advance. This we would then call, a human miracle.

This situation happens often and indeed such an unpredictable idea is what makes life complicated. From this view, we could surely agree with many people's conclusion that life is difficult and sometimes impossible to live with.

> To live with life we need to welcome everything. It means, believing what we see around us is meant for us.

But is life really complicated or do we make it complicated? The answer is, it is human beings who create a complicated or an easy life. If we want to live well, we need to decide that we will not limit ourselves to doing only what we want. To live with life we need to welcome everything. It means, believing what we see around us is meant for us. Believing what we have is meant for us. Believing that whatever situations we face, if we welcome them, we will solve many problems of selfishness and develop an unselfish, good personality. Even though this process may make us suffer sometimes, it is worth welcoming life because we will at least leave our self centered way of life behind.

Living in the Present

Tragically, fear of suffering causes most people to start to dream about life. When we create dreams, it means we no longer live with life or with physical events, we only live with our minds. We create an idea or a desire and we only try to fulfill that specific idea or desire. But in this way we are passing life by, like a cloud that floats over the land without realizing how beautiful the land is. We are passing life by without living with it. Perhaps sometimes we might stop and ask ourselves, "What did I really do in my life?" But because it is so scary to look at our reality, we return to the realm of ideas; we create a wish and we fly again.

Or, we can be the kind of person who doesn't have any idea or wish, a person who just lives the same lifestyle every day and who makes sure that nothing disturbs his way of life. If by accident something happens differently, out of his routine, this person will try to do anything to reject that event.

Through these two descriptions we can see one person is living above the Earth with many ideas and without ever looking at the physical reality, and the other is trying to keep everything the same way forever. For both, the solution is to welcome and to digest life as it comes. And, if they can do so, they will find themselves saying that they love life.

Therefore, I want to ask you to live day by day from now on. To live fully every day we cannot look at the past. We need to learn to forget about what happened yesterday. We need to say to our mind that yesterday doesn't exist anymore, only today exists. This is very difficult to achieve.

> To live fully every day we cannot look at the past. We need to say to our mind that yesterday doesn't exist anymore, only today exists.

Men and women have different ways of approaching life. Women tend to like to bring back memories. In their mind they like to recreate the way it used to be with the hope of experiencing the same feelings again. This happens especially when they go through a difficult moment in their life. Men have a different problem. They will not look to the past in order to escape the present. They will look to the future instead. They will project their minds to some time in the future in order to feel better. This is why they will say, tomorrow will be better.

Both men and women don't know how to live with life. Both use their particular characteristics to escape the present. This is a tragedy. If yesterday doesn't exist anymore, we must also say tomorrow doesn't exist, only today exists. We need to learn to live in the present time with all that we are.

In some religious viewpoints there is always hope in the future. This is good compared with some other religions that teach that people are destined to remain the same or that everything has already been written and cannot be changed one iota. Still, because we want to live today, it is better to say tomorrow doesn't exist. We need to live minute by minute, and based on what we do with our lives each day, we will discover new flavors. If we live with concentration day by day, the effect is that we will become realistic and exciting persons.

So, are we going to continue to dream and pass over the physical world, decreasing in our growth to the point where we see no more hope and are depressed most of the time? What is a true man and a true woman, in other words, a divine man and a divine woman? They know that what they do today will define their destiny tomorrow. What is a true nation? It is a nation that believes what it does each day will create the nation of tomorrow. The viewpoint that we create our destiny by how we live today must be used by each individual, each family, each community and each nation. Every day we write our life with our mind and build it with our actions.

Religious people have learned to have faith in God. They tend to wait for a miracle coming from the sky. They hope something will happen by itself and make them feel better. No, it is we who need to make the miracle. We ourselves need to make ourselves good people. We need to be the ones to make the world a nice place by moving forward inch by inch, moment by moment. It is difficult to live this way, because we need to concentrate fully every day. If we can do this, however, we will create ourselves to the point where we will become divine persons.

The First Day of Our Lives

For some people, their philosophy of life is that life is a joke. They start to laugh about anything, hoping in that way they will glide over the different situations that life gives to them. Some others take life as being so serious that if we try to smile at them they think we dishonor the difficult life they went through.

The best way to live life is to keep our focus on our daily lives. In order to do this, we need to keep a fresh viewpoint every single day. This way our life does not become a routine and we will never lose our excitement about life.

In order to remove the past from our mind or to write something new on the pages of our life that is not just a dream, we need to live with an intensity of love stronger than the impact that past events have made upon us. Only such love can make us forget the past. But to have this love we need to learn how to have a fresh viewpoint every day, and that indeed is a miracle.

If this miracle cannot take place inside of us, then we are going to become tired of seeing the same people around us day after day. But if our eyes can look with freshness and purity on every event that composes life, we can live with people a very long time without ever becoming tired of them.

We need to make ourselves good people. We need to be the ones to make the world a nice place by moving forward inch by inch, moment by moment.

In order to be this kind of pure person who can always live in the present moment, we need to find the presence of God's love. We need to invite Him to come with us. Together with Him, who is love, we can live life well with ourselves and with others. Now, can we understand why many of us have difficulty to look at life with joy and happiness?

When our bodies are young, we tend to look towards the future. The more we age, the more we accumulate past years, the more it becomes difficult to look to the future and easier to look to the past. But if we look at people in the present time while keeping all our past memories, we will become disheartened at some point because everything they do resembles our memories, and for this reason we will start to reject people.

When we start to see these events taking place in our minds, it is the beginning of detaching ourselves from the life we were once happy about and the beginning of being pessimistic about the life we once looked upon with optimism. Step by step life becomes an enemy to us and something we feel we have to defend ourselves from.

If we always look to the past, we start to calculate how much we gave and how much we still are giving. By doing so we will no longer be able to see how much people are still giving to us, to the point where we can believe they never gave anything at all to us. Calculating provokes many expectations in us, and after we have created so much unfulfilled desire inside, if these expectations are not fulfilled, we will become negative. In the end we will come to a point where we will totally reject life as well as ourselves.

> Living with God is inviting Him
> into our lives in every event.

All this occurs because we are incapable of keeping our eyes pure and fresh towards life. It is not easy to feel every day is the first day of our lives. To be able to do so we need to incorporate God's principle and God's love in us. Without living our lives with God we cannot live until the end of our lives with an optimistic mind and eyes full of purity. What is living with God? Living with God is living according to God's principle, which is to love, first Him and then others. Living with God is inviting Him into our lives in every event. And, if we decide to love Him and invite Him all the time, we will create many victories and we will experience life as being the deepest miracle. Even though we live for many years, we will still have enthusiasm until the end.

If we live in this way we won't need to reject life anymore, we won't need to review all that we did, we will just need to digest what is happening on a daily basis.

Unite Mind and Body

So I will say, from now on give all your energy to what you live with, and embrace life. This way of life simplifies all confusion and erases all complaints. By now we have come to realize that we have an optimistic and a pessimistic side within us. Our optimistic side makes us look ahead, which symbolizes our mind, and our pessimistic side makes us look behind, which symbolizes our body. It is only by living in the present that we can unite both the mind and the body together. By living in the future we project our mind in advance of what our body is dealing with. By living in the past we project our mind toward the memories of our body and in this way we will think beforehand that we won't be able to do something. In both cases our mind and our body are in different places.

If we look at the memories of our body, at what we already did, we will feel depressed. Let's say we live with someone who often reminds us about everything they gave or did for us. I believe after a while we will no longer want to receive anything from this person. This can be the case when our parents served us meals for ten years and every time they cooked for us they reminded us about how many meals they had already cooked for us. At some point we will feel guilty to eat their meals and eventually we will decide to no longer eat in their home. We will end up buying our own food. This happens in families where the parents calculate everything, in other words, where the parents are always looking at the past.

We therefore must not remember the past if we want to be persons who can love unconditionally. We need to give and forget what we gave.

We therefore must not remember the past if we want to be persons who can love unconditionally. We need to give and forget what we gave. Many times we give to people so that they will respond to us in the future. Then, when the future arrives and they don't respond, we begin to calculate and through that our expectations transform into negativity. For example, if the parents are constantly reminding their children what they did for them, it means they start to expect something from their children. The effect on the one who listens might be to feel that he or she is a burden to the parents and this child will begin to make plans to leave the house. As parents I think it is good to occasionally tell our children what we did for them so they can realize nothing is free, nothing comes without effort and therefore they can appreciate more deeply what was given to them. But there is a big difference between telling them sometimes and telling them every day.

If we start to observe ourselves giving, we will begin to calculate everything in terms of how much money, time or effort we gave to someone. Eventually we will become depressed, especially if we try to check if the person gave back to us equally. We will say, "Oh, I did so much but nobody responded," to the point where we will stop to give. From that moment we are going to lose hope. Hope represents our mind. We will then turn towards the memories of our body. This will make us choose the road of selfishness, which maybe we never believed we would ever do.

The best way to live is to destroy all of our expectations and to forget about our past. Look instead at the present time and do the best we can with all our mind, body and heart. Surely it is difficult to give unconditionally, but nevertheless we need to strive to become this kind of person, as it is the purpose of our life to become a person who can give without calculating. Living this way will create joy inside us and with time we will create a good personality, eventually graduating to a new level, to become what we call, a divine person.

The same as we have dreams, God also has big dreams for the future, one of them being to build the Kingdom of Heaven on Earth as well as in Heaven. He is also a God of the past. He keeps some record of history for us to know where we came from and to learn to be grateful for what we have now. But especially He is a God of the present. This is why every moment of history is written differently and is constantly changing. Because God has this nature, if we can start to live with life He can always live with us and can create something new through us. Therefore I can say that the person who can live in the present will meet the living God. This person will become a realistic person and will surely conclude in the end that God is alive.

Living in Duality with Others

The question then is, how to live fully in the present every day? To live fully we need to live for someone else besides ourselves. It is the other person who helps us to live in the present, because in order to live for others we need to concentrate on what they wish and not on what we wish. Then, because we are completely focusing on harmonizing with others, we can save ourselves from having illusions or delusions about life. We cannot always dream about the future and we cannot just contemplate the past.

As we learn to live with and for others, we will discover new strengths in us, since this way of life obliges us to unite our mind and our body. By living in the present others will become close to us and through this foundation God's love can come with us in the same moment. This is one of the major reasons He created human beings to live next to each other.

But because it is difficult to be focused each moment, we cannot constantly live with people and therefore we start to choose to isolate ourselves from them. However, if we want God to be part of us, if we want Him to live with us, we need to live in duality with others. For us to create love we need a subject and an object. So, when we reject someone or we cannot live with someone, we also reject love, in other words, we reject God.

For example, we sometimes say to ourselves that we don't want to be disturbed. Then, if somebody or some event comes close to our life, we will experience so much rejection within us. We will find ourselves saying to our friends, "Why do you bother me?" or to our children, "You are giving me a hard time." But, worst of all, if rejecting the present moment becomes our tradition, in other words, if we do so for a long period of time, we will start to eventually reject ourselves, to the point where we will feel that we should never have been born.

> We cannot always dream about the future and we cannot just contemplate the past.

Do we want to become this kind of man or woman? I guess we will all say no. The other option is to become a realistic being. Regardless this can be difficult from time to time, it is a wonderful and exciting way of life, and in the process of living this way we will experience the presence of our Creator, God.

So far many of us live alone even though other people are next to us, and we are always afraid of being in despair instead of living in joy and happiness with the love of God. So, let's live life, accept what comes to us. Don't just study life, live with it. Don't philosophize about what you see, or panic when you see something new is going to happen, just go slowly inside each new event.

Don't just study life, live with it. Don't philosophize about what you see, or panic when you see something new is going to happen, just go slowly inside each new event.

The beginning is maybe difficult, because every part of us is challenged. It is not bad to be challenged, instead it is a chance to grow ourselves. It is similar to when we experience extreme weather. Our body does not withdraw when it faces this new event, but instead it tries to adjust itself to live with what is extreme. This is an amazing aspect of our body.

Many people panic just to hear a new idea. Why worry about a new idea before it is even realized? Why do we put our mind into turmoil before we are even faced with an actual event? If our mind panics, we will start to feel strong emotions in ourselves, then we will start to lose control of ourselves and reject any idea before it can be carried out. This phenomenon takes place because we don't trust life, or more concretely, we don't trust what is coming to us. In other words, we don't trust present events as part of our life.

So, what should we do if we find a new situation coming to us? First, we need to not worry about it until it comes to us in reality. In the moment we face it, we can think about how to deal with it and try to find a way to harmonize with it. If we worry about a situation even before it comes to us physically, we will find one hundred excuses why it cannot work out.

Today there are many philosophies that teach us to just focus on ourselves and on our own situation. These philosophies provoke destruction, despair and eventually revolution, since they encourage selfishness. Then there are many theologies that make us forget the present and ask us to focus on the future, as far away as eternity. They also do not bring forth something better, because they make us irresponsible towards being physically present in life.

We are Made to Look Outside Us

Therefore, please accept to live life where you are and with the people around you. If every day you use your mind and body to live, your life will not just be a 'life' but a 'life of love'.

Loving is accepting what we see and harmonizing with what we receive. Accepting whatever is coming to us is the most beautiful talent we can develop. It permits us to create a round personality that can adjust itself to the many different situations of life.

If we complain even before we confront a new situation or once we are in a situation, we accelerate the separation of our mind and body, and without realizing it we stop living in the moment. As a result, our mind wants to be in a different place than our body is. For example, our mind is dreaming about home while our body is at work, or we are with our friends and suddenly our mind wants to be in another place. All these situations make us abandon our reality. But if we try to keep our mind where our body is, we will establish a foundation of unity between our mind and body, which will make us feel peace inside us.

> If every day you use your mind
> and body to live, your life will not
> just be a 'life' but a 'life of love'.

When our mind starts to have some new wish or we project our mind somewhere else, to a place we believe to be better, it is because we become tired of the situation we are in. Then our mind will travel to a land of the future or a land of the past. And, if we allow our mind to settle in one of these two lands, whichever it may be, we will start to either dwell on what we did or think about what we want to do.

Regardless it is difficult to stay in the present moment, if we want to develop our personality, we need to put our heart and our enthusiasm voluntarily into what we do and into the people we live with. Then our mind and body can unite and we can experience God's love through that union.

Physically, we are not made to look at ourselves. If we consider our face, we will realize that our eyes are made to look outside of us, not inside, and our ears are made to listen to what is outside of us, not inside. In order to live fully with the people who are next to us, we need to look straight at them and to listen to them. To do this, we need to focus our mind on the physical person in front of us and not focus inside of us. When our mind separates itself from our body, we cannot really see the person well. Due to this, after a while we will find ourselves rejecting the person's attitude or his or her way of doing things.

It is because we have a tendency to not like the physical side of life that our mind starts to leave our body. When this happens, we are forced to turn around inside our mind and create many dreams, illusions and concepts. After a person discovers this world of the mind, he will surely prefer it to his physical reality, because in the world of ideas everything looks cleaner, more beautiful and easier to do than in the world of reality.

Realists and Idealists

Human beings also have a tendency to idealize reality. Many times they do this within a group of people, preaching about the hope for a better world in the future. But along with their idealistic theory they tend to reject the daily life that they are faced with and regardless of their optimism, they do not show enthusiasm for people outside their group, because they feel these others do not share their viewpoint.

There are also many people who measure life based only on what they can see with their physical eyes or based on the external talents people have. We usually call them materialists. They see life according to what is productive secularly. In some ways they are the ones who seem to be more realistic, but when we look at them more closely we can observe they compare their lives with the lives of their neighbors, and most of the time they believe they are more miserable than their neighbors, to the point where they never believe what they have is enough.

Surely both kinds of people are missing one aspect of life, and they are in conflict with each other as well, because they each realize the other is lacking something. This conflict exists between people and also within individuals, between their minds and their bodies. Because of this conflict between the mind and the body within individuals, we can observe two major groups of people in the world. One group stands on the side of the mind and promotes spiritual values, but they deny the necessity of matter by blaming the extravagance of the materialists for the problems of the world. The other group, the materialists, claim that religious people promote poverty and ignorance because they reject the physical needs of people in the name of saving their souls.

If we can look at the situation from an objective point of view, we realize there are needs on both the physical and the spiritual sides. Therefore, by listening to each other, both kinds of people can learn what they are missing in order to create a world where a soul can grow and, as well, where there can be a splendid physical environment.

But usually, if we stand on one side, we want to eliminate the group that stands on the other side in order to promote what we believe is most important. This event has happened many times throughout history. At certain times religion was in the leading position, at other times materialism took over.

We have never seen both philosophies becoming one through all of our history. Regardless there were some cultures that tolerated the idea of the existence of a soul, it only remained as an idea that was not part of their daily affairs. Because no one considered the realm of spiritual values and the realm of material values should become one, this conflict continues even today. We see brothers and sisters or husbands and wives divided because they each stand for a different side. Where does this originate? It originates inside ourselves, when we deny either our mind or our body.

Welcome Events Instead of Trying to Escape from Them

Nowadays, people don't use religion as often to escape reality, but they have found other techniques. They read books, watch television and movies, or play games that transport them to a different place or draw them into a love scene or an action scene created by the writer or the producer. When we read a book or watch a movie, we start to imagine ourselves to be the person in that story, because this creates excitement in us. We find ourselves switching between the different characters of the story. The problem is that we develop a lot of imagination and many desires that have nothing to do with the reality of our lives. Of course we are created to have imagination, but all these stories can fill up our minds to the point they prevent us from accepting and fully living our own lives.

> If we want to experience love, we need to create a founda- tion for love inside ourselves.

The emotions people create in this kind of situation, like anticipation or longing, are not love. We read romances, as well as science fiction, thrillers and other genres, because we wish to have a more dramatic personality. We choose a type of story that is connected to our internal self. Regardless we experience romantic feelings by reading our novel, the reality is that if we want to experience love, we need to create a foundation for love inside ourselves. This foundation for love demands that we engage in interaction with the people who are around us.

So, first we need to accept whatever we are given. What we do with what we are given will influence what will happen to us. In other words, we are the cause of what happens to us. Let's use an example. Let's say we are indifferent to people, then sooner or later, people will also be indifferent to us. If we judge them, they will judge us. But if we live life fully with all our mind, body and heart, people will welcome us, because we ourselves are full of life. If we are true with others, they will be true with us. It is we who choose the cause and create the effect of our lives.

If we ask various people what life is, we will discover they each perceive life in different ways according to who they are. If we don't want to open our eyes to see who we really are, we create the tendency to dream. This is because, when we cannot accept a certain situation, we realize we are not the person we thought we were. We then reject the situation that makes us feel incapable or inadequate. Instead, it would be better for us to stay humble and to learn to live with the situation that presents itself to us.

If we can keep this kind of humble attitude, we will realize that life is not as difficult as it seems to be and we will be able to confront a multitude of so-called problems. If we live this way, we will become divine persons. And, as we drive ourselves to become divine beings, we will start to feel less fearful of life. We won't try to find ways to escape life through creating dreams or illusions, and we won't bring despair upon ourselves any more.

Due to our imaginations, many of us cannot interact harmoniously with our wife, our husband, or our children. We project ourselves inside our imagination and consequently we reject the people around us. But if we want to have love, we need our wife, our husband, our children and other people, because they help us to discover and to change ourselves. It is with them we can create love and happiness. Contrary to that, many times we act as if we don't need anybody. By placing value on our independence, we turn to ourselves and we create our own reality according to our imagination and beliefs, which are unlimited because everything just happens in our mind.

What is the Kingdom of Heaven?

The question is, do we want to be divine persons or do we want to dream about something wonderful that makes us only appear to be divine persons? Do we want to create our divine selves, the fulfillment of the purpose of our lives? If so, we need to focus on everything we do with our whole mind and body, in other words, be interested in what we do, especially when something is not familiar to us or doesn't attract us so much. We should remove all the concepts that come to our mind like an avalanche and focus on what we do with our full being, then one day we will like what we do.

By putting all our heart in all we do, we will create an ideal world, and we will be in the Kingdom of Heaven.

By focusing on life, we will forget about the dream of being an ideal person one day, or about an ideal world or the Kingdom of Heaven coming one day. By putting all our heart in all we do, we will create an ideal world, and we will be in the Kingdom of Heaven.

Therefore, please don't promote dreams but deal with life. Maybe we feel if we don't have a dream, then what is left of life? Just depression? Maybe this is why it is difficult for us to stop dreaming. But if we don't remove our dreams and live in the moment, our dreams will remove themselves from us, step by step. How many of us already lost the dream of having a nice family or gave up other ideals, because we became disillusioned? Others never even begin to dream. They say, "Look, I am realistic about myself. I know I have many problems and I also know that I cannot do anything about them."

Forget about whatever you are not or whatever accusation you feel; just remember that in order to live in the Kingdom of Heaven you need to live for others. This is the law of the universe.

In both cases we are predicting the future. But the answer to both examples is to unite our mind and body in the present situation and through this we will develop our heart. In the moment we focus on living for others, the love of God can be projected inside us. If everyone does this, I absolutely believe the Kingdom of Heaven can be established inside of us and outside of us.

Maybe you never realized it, but in the moment you give something to somebody, you start to feel something passing through you. It is because in that moment you open yourself and you can receive love according to how much you give. This is a universal law. For this reason you need someone to give to and to receive from in your life, so love can move in and out. This love will create a miracle in you—it will seal your mind and body together. This has to be achieved before you leave this Earth so that you can breathe the love of God forever.

So, can you still believe that you can live just centered on yourself? If you focus on yourself, you focus on what is inside you, on depression, emptiness and a sense of lack of value. Maybe you have a high awareness of your incompleteness. I will say, forget about whatever you are not or whatever accusation you feel; just remember that in order to live in the Kingdom of Heaven you need to live for others. This is the law of the universe.

Until we can accomplish what we are made for, we cannot truly feel that we are a good person even though others compliment us. The best way to achieve a sense of goodness is to make ourselves beautiful for some-body else. Then that somebody will be so happy to be our friend or to have us as wife or husband. He or she will want to protect and support us in any way and God Himself will also be happy about us.

Create a Miracle

So, let's live for life and for love. Don't fight life, don't argue about life. If you fight what comes to you, life will abandon you. If you argue with life, it will make you confused. Don't try to challenge life, because you will finish your existence tired and in despair. Don't focus on winning, focus on accepting everything, and then you will win.

> Don't focus on winning, focus on accepting everything, and then you will win.

When we are discontented about life, our only accomplishment will be to endure life. And if somebody asks us what life was for us, surely we will consider ourselves to be victims of society. If we see ourselves this way, we close ourselves to anything that exists around us and because of that nothing can nourish us. And so, nothing of our divine self can come out of us.

So, let's digest society, digest life, be open to what comes to us. The same as the darkness of the night disappears when the light of the new day is coming, the darkness that pessimism creates inside of us will disappear when we open ourselves to the life around us.

The same as the Sun has the power to awaken the planet to life, God's love can also awaken us as we welcome every situation in our lives. The same as the warmth of the Sun evaporates the rain from the Earth, God's love warms our souls and makes us forget whatever we went through.

If we are open to life, we can receive God's love and therefore we can deal with many situations that look im-

possible to go through. To begin, we need to make ourselves objects to the love of God, which is in the position
of subject. It is the same as the Sun standing in the position of subject toward the Earth, which is its object. So, I
can say, if we can live fully with life, we will open the door
for God's love.

*By living for others, God's love
will be close to you all the time.*

So, please, live well with all your body, mind, and
heart. By living for others, God's love will be close to
you all the time and assist you in whatever you want
to accomplish. You won't even need to ask something
from Him, you will just need to observe yourself well—
observe if you are living according to the principle of
God's love. If you do so, He will give all the love He has
to you.

Remember, by accepting whatever we are involved
with, love will begin to be with us. This is extremely different from a life without love, as we well know from our
experience. Everything was made to create love. Every
day is made as an opportunity to harmonize with different situations, which we usually identify as 'problems'.
These so-called problems come all the time because we
can't stop new events from happening, especially if we
live with human beings. But the more we can live well
with each event, the more there will be a miracle taking
place inside of us. We will create ourselves with a round

and lovely character that looks similar to God's character, and we will therefore create love between God and us.

Unite with Life

I hope you will use yourself to live well. Accept to learn new things in your life. Use your imagination to live with the situations that open themselves to you, instead of using it to leave or to accuse the reality of life. Don't block yourself with negative thoughts.

This miracle can only happen if you decide to love. Learn to be flexible in every situation that comes close to you. Don't fight life but challenge your qualification to love. Be grateful everywhere no matter what. Accept problems; it is because of them that you can learn to develop your heart of love.

> Accept problems; it is because
> of them that you can learn to
> develop your heart of love.

It is difficult to know whether we live life well, but I can assure you, if we live with and not against life, we are living well. Remember, God created life for love. Love is more important than life, but we cannot have love if we don't accept life. God created life so that love can explode inside and between every human being, especially between man and woman, between parents and children and between God and humankind.

When we reject life, we reject love at the same time. This is the tragedy of humankind. But if we unite with life, then we will unite with love. This is the greatest miracle we can make for God.

In school we receive a secular education, but nobody has developed a school where we can graduate with a degree in knowing how to live life. Yet without this kind of degree, we will not know how to live well in our adult life and surely not in our next life. This is a major problem we are not aware of and yet we all become victims of, because we only have some kind of dream for our next life but no training for it.

To live well we don't need to think so deeply. We just need to make our mind accept each situation as it comes. The first difficulty is to make our mind accept life when it wants to reject it. The second difficulty is to make our body fulfill what we made our mind agree with. As we can see, the problem of not being able to live well comes from our mind and our body being against life. If we can make them agree to want to harmonize with life, we will begin to know what real love is.

So, do you know the Sun is shining today? Did you see the Sun and did you appreciate it? If it is raining, can you also be fascinated with the rain? This is part of the attitude you need in order to live with life. Are you grateful to live or are you complaining about life? What you choose is either against or for true love.

Now, are you going to accept what is around you: the weather, your work, the people? More than that, can you accept yourselves? You are also part of life. By accepting to live with yourselves and with the people around you, you will discover true love in each other; in other words, you will discover God.

Personally, I would like you to become part of life, from now on until forever. So, may life be your friend so that true love can be with you.